HEINEMANN STATE STUDIES

People of
Illinois

Andrew Santella

© 2003 Reed Educational & Professional Publishing
Published by Heinemann Library,
an imprint of Reed Educational & Professional
Publishing, Chicago, Illinois

Customer Service 888-454-2279

Visit our website at www.heinemannlibrary.com

Designed by Heinemann Library
Page layout by Depke Design
Printed and bound in the United States by Lake
Book Manufacturing, Inc.

07 06 05 04 03
10 9 8 7 6 5 4 3 2 1

**Library of Congress
Cataloging-in-Publication Data**
Santella, Andrew.
 People of Illinois / by Andrew Santella.
  v. cm. -- (State studies)
Includes bibliographical references (p. 47) and
index.
Contents: The first people in Illinois -- Americans
move west to Illinois -- Immigrants from Europe --
Twentieth-century growth --Illinois in the twenty-
first century -- Illinois achievers.
 ISBN 1-40340-010-5 (HC), 1-40340-571-9 (PbK)
 1. Illinois--History--Juvenile literature. 2. Illinois--
Population--Juvenile literature. 3. Ethnology--Illi-
nois--Juvenile literature. [1. Illinois--History. 2. Illi-
nois--Population. 3. Ethnology--Illinois.] I. Title. II.
State studies (Heinemann Library (Firm))
 F541.3 .S27 2002
 977.3--dc21

                                        2002000799

Acknowledgments
The author and publishers are grateful to the
following for permission to reproduce copyright
material:

Cover photographs by (TL-TR): Chicago Historical
Society; John H. White; Robert Lifson/Heinemann
Library; Moffett/Chicago Historical Society;
(bottom) Daniel Lain/Corbis

p. 4 Courtesy of Cahokia Mounds State Historic
Site; pp. 5, 29 maps.com/ Heinemann Library;
p. 6 "Man Who Tracks, a Chief," by George Catlin.
Gift of Mrs. Joseph Harrison, Jr., Smithsonian
American Art Museum, Washington, D.C. /Art
Resource; p. 7, 14, 16, 39T, 42L Corbis; p. 8
Hulton Getty; pp. 10, 18R, 22B, 23B, 24B Robert
Lifson/Heinemann Library; pp. 11, 20, 37T, 42B
Chicago Historical Society; pp. 12, 17 The Granger
Collection, NY; pp. 13T, 34, 42R Stock Montage,
Inc.; pp. 13B, 18L, 19T, 35, 38, 44 Bettmann/
Corbis; p. 15T Courtesy Augustana College;
pp. 15B, 30 Illinois Department of Commerce and
Community Affairs; p. 19B Courtesy of Fermilab;
p. 21T The Chicago Daily Defender; p. 21B, 45T
John H. White; p. 22T Charles Bennett/AP/Wide
World Photos; p. 23T Mexican Fine Arts Center
Museum; p. 24T Courtesy Chicago Symphony
Orchestra; p. 25 Skidmore, Owings & Merrill LLP;
p. 26 C.C. Lockwood/Bruce Coleman, Inc.;
p. 27 Mark E. Gibson; pp. 28, 33T Heinemann
Library; p. 31 Courtesy of the City of Bloomington;
p. 32 David Derr; p. 33B Debra P.Hershkowitz/
Bruce Coleman, Inc.; p. 36 Courtesy office of
Senator Hillary Clinton; p. 37B R. Varin, Paris,
1930/Chicago Historical Society; p. 39B NASA;
p. 40 Tim O'Dell/NBA Photos; p. 41 Chicago
Historical Society; p. 43 Courtesy Ronald Reagan
Library; p. 45B Mitchell Gerber/Corbis

Special thanks to Tom Schwartz of the Illinois
Historic Preservation Agency, for his expert help
and advice on the series.

Every effort has been made to contact copyright
holders of any material reproduced in this book.
Any omissions will be rectified in subsequent
printings if notice is given to the publisher.

Some words are shown in bold, **like this.**
You can find out what they mean by looking
in the glossary.

Contents

The First People in Illinois

The people of Illinois make it a truly interesting and diverse state. Many different groups of people have come to Illinois over many years and have created that **diversity.** They came to Illinois for many reasons. Some came to farm the rich land. Others came seeking freedom to follow their religious beliefs. Still others looked for jobs in the factories and mines of Illinois. These people came from all over the world, and they have all made their own contributions to the state's history.

PALEO-INDIANS

The first people to live in Illinois were Paleo-Indians. They arrived in Illinois about 15,000 years ago. Over thousands of years, different groups of people settled in Illinois. Over time, each of these groups disappeared. They were wiped out by enemies, disease, starvation, or

People of the Mississippian Culture built large mounds around C.E. 1000. The largest of those mounds, Monks Mound (below, background), can still be climbed today.

Illinois

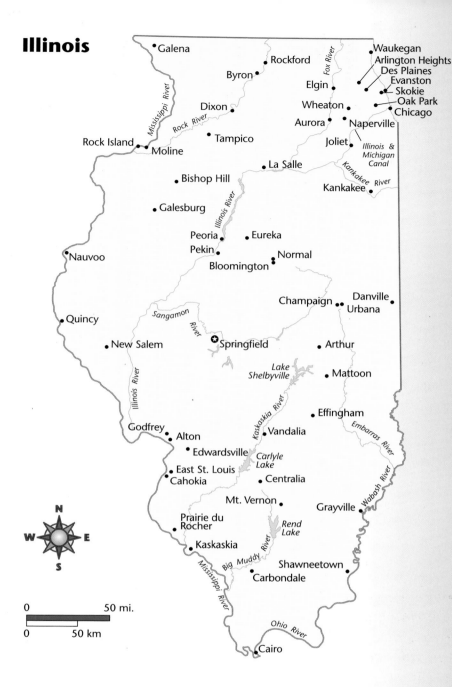

even the loss of trees. Each of these groups was replaced by others that followed. In about 1000 B.C.E., people of the **Woodland Culture** became Illinois's first growers of corn. People of the **Mississippian Culture** began living in Illinois around C.E. 900. In about C.E. 1000, those people built the first large towns in Illinois. The largest of their towns, near the present-day city of Collinsville, Illinois, was home to 15,000 people.

Around 1400, a new group of Native Americans began living in Illinois. These were the tribes of the Illinois Confederacy, or the Illiniwek. Illiniwek, roughly translated, means "the men," or "the people." Illinois is actually the term the French used to describe the Native Americans they first encountered, and that term has lasted to this day. A confederacy is a group of tribes that agree to protect each other from common enemies. The tribes of the Illinois Confederacy shared a common language called Algonquin. The Confederacy included the Peoria, Kaskaskia, Tamaroa, Cahokia, and Michigamia tribes, among others.

This is an 1830 painting of Pah-me-cow-e-tah (Man Who Tracks), a Peoria chief. The Peoria were part of the Illinois Confederacy.

The people of the Illinois Confederacy ate the plants and animals that lived in the Illinois landscape. They grew corn and pumpkins and hunted for **bison.** In fact, their homeland was so rich that the Illinois lost much of it to other Native American peoples, as well as to white settlers, once they arrived. In the 1600s and 1700s, Sauk, Fox, Kickapoo, and Potowatomi people all moved into territory once held by the Illinois Confederacy. The Iroquois people also invaded Illinois territory. The Iroquois were the most feared Native American warriors east of the Mississippi River. They occupied vast lands stretching from New England to the Great Lakes. With guns purchased from English and Dutch traders along the Hudson River in New York, they sometimes waged war on the Illinois and drove them off their land.

EUROPEANS COME TO ILLINOIS

In 1673, people from Europe made their way to Illinois for the first time. The first Europeans to come to Illinois were Frenchmen. In the late 1600s and early 1700s, they built churches, **forts,** and villages alongside the rivers of Illinois. At this time, Illinois tribes still lived in the area. The French came to trade with those Native Americans, expand the fur trade, and introduce Native Americans to the **Catholic** faith. The first French explorers to reach Illinois were Jacques Marquette and Louis Jolliet.

Jacques Marquette

Jacques Marquette (1637–1675) was a Catholic **missionary** from France. A missionary is a person who travels to spread his or her religious faith. Marquette journeyed deep into the interior of North America to live with Native Americans. He built a church and mission near St. Ignace, Michigan, far from other French settlements. There he met Native Americans from Illinois who told him about a great river that flowed south to the sea. They were describing the Mississippi River. With the help of Native American guides, Marquette and a mapmaker named Louis Jolliet became the first Europeans to travel most of the length of the Mississippi River. In 1674, Marquette returned to Illinois to build a mission. However, he became ill and died before he could complete the mission.

To win the friendship of the Illinois Confederacy, French explorers told the Native Americans they would protect them from their Iroquois enemies. The French built **forts** along the Illinois and Mississippi Rivers. Their Native American trading partners built their villages nearby. However, the French were not able to keep their promise to protect their Native American friends. The tribes of the Illinois Confederacy were driven into the southern tip of Illinois, or south across the Missouri River (located in what is today the state of Missouri). Disease and warfare destroyed entire tribes. Before the French came to Illinois, about 20,000 Native Americans lived in the area.

The French were the first Europeans to build villages in Illinois. This is a drawing of a house (below) built by French settlers at Kaskaskia in the mid–1600s. It was built with wood.

The French and Slavery

The French brought the first Africans to Illinois as slaves around 1720. In 1752, there were 446 African slaves in Illinois. French laws required slave owners to educate their slaves in the **Catholic** faith. They also made the slaves follow French **customs.** Some slaves still tried to keep their own religious beliefs. They had to do so in secret, however. A slave caught practicing an African religion could be severely punished.

By 1700, there were just 6,000. By 1768, there were only about 2,200 Native Americans living in Illinois.

Towns soon grew around the churches and forts that the French built in Illinois. The French founded Kaskaskia in 1703, and Prairie du Rocher in 1732. At that time, the French lived in log houses. Each house had several rooms, with one large main room where the cooking was done over a large fire. In some French villages, farm fields were kept separate from the homes. A fence protected the fields, which were organized in long strips, usually along a river. The fields were long and narrow so that farmers plowing the fields wouldn't have to turn their plows around as often.

The French lost control of Illinois after England won the **French and Indian War,** which took place from 1754 to 1763. England made little effort to settle Illinois. Between 1763 and 1778, the population of Illinois actually decreased. Some French settlers moved west across the Mississippi River. Others continued to live near Peoria and Kaskaskia, since the British did not have a strong presence there.

Moving West to Illinois

After the American Revolution (1775–1783), Illinois became a United States **territory.** The next large group of settlers to move into Illinois were American settlers from southern states like Virginia, Kentucky, and Tennessee. They began coming in the early 1800s, and helped settle the area in the 1820s and 1830s. They settled mainly in southern Illinois, along the Ohio, Mississippi, and other major rivers. The flat, open prairies of Illinois looked strange to them, which is why they settled the wooded areas along the rivers. The nearby trees provided wood for fences and fuel.

At first the treeless prairies looked strange to settlers. They stayed near the woods of Illinois until John Deere's 1837 steel plow helped them cut through tough prairie grass roots.

Land of Lincoln

Abraham Lincoln was part of the wave of southerners who moved to Illinois. He was born in Kentucky in 1809. With his mother and father, he moved to Indiana in 1816. The Lincoln family then moved to Illinois in 1830. They were searching for good, cheap farmland. Young Abraham's uncle had already moved to Illinois and told the family about the good land there. The Lincolns settled on a farm about ten miles from Decatur, which was still a small frontier village at the time. The Lincoln farm was on the north bank of the Sangamon River. Young Abraham used an axe to cut wood to make a fence for the farm. Frontier people called this railsplitting. Thirty years later, when Lincoln became president, people still called him Railsplitter Abe.

Present-day Randolph, Monroe, and St. Clair Counties, in the southwest part of the state, were the first areas of Illinois to be settled by Americans. In the early years of the 1800s, Illinois grew rapidly. In 1800, there were just 2,450 people in Illinois. When Illinois became a state in 1818, about 35,000 people lived there. Most of them lived in the southern part of the state. The biggest towns were Shawneetown, Edwardsville, and Kaskaskia. As more settlers arrived, the last Native Americans in Illinois were driven from their land.

NORTHERNERS IN ILLINOIS

In 1825, the Erie Canal opened in the state of New York. Even though it was far away, it affected Illinois. It was

River Travel

To early settlers, the rivers of Illinois were like highways. People traveled down the Ohio, Wabash, Big Muddy, and Embarras Rivers to get to their new homes in Illinois. One of the most popular ways to travel on rivers was in flatboats (right). Flatboats were large, flat-bottomed boats designed for river travel. Settlers used flatboats to send their farm goods to market, too. Flatboats carried corn, pork, flour, and other produce down the Mississippi River to buyers as far away as New Orleans, Louisiana.

now possible for goods to travel across the Great Lakes, through the Erie Canal to the Hudson River in the state of New York, and then all the way to New York City and the Atlantic Ocean. This meant that farm produce grown in Illinois could more easily reach buyers in the East. Because of this, the Erie Canal helped bring money into Illinois.

Another group of settlers began moving to Illinois once the Erie Canal was finished. These were people from New England and New York, sometimes called Yankees. Most of them settled in northern and central Illinois.

Like the Southerners who had come before, Yankees were attracted to the cheap land available in Illinois. The two groups were very different, however. Their biggest difference had to do with what they believed about slavery. The Southerners came from states where slavery was legal, and most of them were used to the practice. Some Northerners in Illinois worked to outlaw slavery completely. Many of the Illinoisans who worked to outlaw slavery were Yankees from New England and New York. Even though Illinois entered the United States as a free state in 1818, some early state laws were designed to **discriminate** against African Americans and prevent slaves traveling through the state from trying to escape.

RELIGIOUS GROUPS

In 1839, members of the **Mormon** religion came to Illinois. They came from Missouri, where they had trouble with hostile neighbors. They thought they would find a safe place in Illinois. They settled near Quincy, on the western border of central Illinois. Residents helped them survive the first winter. The Mormons soon settled in their own city, called Nauvoo. It was governed by the church's leaders. The church's founder, Joseph Smith, was the city's mayor, commander of the local militia, and editor of the town newspaper. By 1845, so many new Mormons had moved to Nauvoo that it became the

Elijah Parish Lovejoy

Elijah Parish Lovejoy (1802–1837) moved to Illinois from Maine to publish a newspaper for the **Presbyterian Church.** He voiced his antislavery views in the paper, the *Alton Observer.* Those views made him very unpopular with his Alton neighbors. Three times mobs destroyed his printing press, and three times he replaced it with a new one. Lovejoy was finally killed by one of the mobs on November 7, 1837, while defending the warehouse that held his printing press. His death brought greater attention to the issue of slavery and brought more support for **abolition.**

Joseph Smith (left) led the Mormons to Illinois. They built Nauvoo, which became the largest city in the state by 1845.

Advertising Illinois

Why was Illinois such a popular destination for people from all over the world? Partly because these new settlers read pleasing descriptions of Illinois in books and magazines. For example, a German traveler named Ferdinand Ernst published a book about his travels in Illinois in 1819. In this book, Ernst described what he had seen in Illinois: "[N]o more inviting thing can be imagined for a stranger than to settle here and to live in this abundance of nature. He needs nothing more than to put the plow once into these grassy plains, which are for the most part quite level, and his fields are splendid with the richest fruits and the most abundant harvests." With descriptions like this, it's no wonder settlers came to Illinois!

largest city in Illinois. As Mormons grew more powerful in Illinois, their neighbors tried to drive them out. In 1844, an angry mob killed Joseph Smith. Two years later, the Mormons began leaving Illinois to set up a new settlement in Utah.

The first Swedes came to Illinois to escape religious persecution, among other reasons. The Swedish government

The Mormon Temple in Nauvoo (right) was completed in 1846, just months before the Mormons left for Utah. It was destroyed by fire in 1848.

was connected to the State **Lutheran Church.** Until 1858, people who practiced another religion in Sweden could be fined, put in jail, or kicked out of the country. A group of Swedes moved to Bishop Hill, in northwest Illinois, in 1846, and set up their own colony there. That colony did not survive, but other Swedes founded churches throughout Illinois, as well as Augustana College, which is now located in Rock Island, Illinois.

Augustana College (above) was originally founded in Chicago in 1860 by Swedish immigrants. It moved to Rock Island in 1875.

In 1831, Amish people from Switzerland settled along the Illinois River in Woodford, Tazewell, and Bureau Counties. In 1865, a group of Amish people settled in Arthur, and they still live happily there today. The Amish believe in living a simple, **Christian** life, based on working hard and avoiding unnecessary material goods. Their traditional rules ban the use of electricity and telephones. Instead of driving cars, they travel in horse-drawn wagons. Amish farmers use horses to work their fields. About 4,200 Amish still live this simple life in Illinois.

Arthur, Illinois, is still home to a thriving Amish community. Amish there still use horses to travel (left) and plow their farm fields. Their traditional rules ban the use of modern electrical equipment.

Immigrants from Europe

Large groups of **immigrants** from other countries began coming to Illinois around 1850. The largest groups came from Germany and Ireland. They often came to avoid **famine.** Many of these people helped build the new railroads that were stretching across Illinois. These railroads helped make Illinois a crossroads for a growing nation. In 1850, about 16,000 immigrants came to Illinois from Germany. About 13,000 came from Ireland the same year. Railroads carried new settlers to growing towns on the prairie. Cities like Bloomington, Champaign, and Mattoon began as railroad station stops. Between 1850 and 1890, about 10,000 miles (16,093 kilometers) of railroad track was laid in Illinois, much of it by immigrants.

THE IMMIGRANT'S LIFE

More European immigrants came to Illinois to work in the steel industry and meatpacking plants in the late

Many immigrants worked in meatpacking plants and the Chicago Union Stockyards (right). The Union Stockyards processed 2 million animals each year by 1870. At that time, waste from the animals flowed into the Chicago River and then into Lake Michigan.

In the late 1800s and early 1900s, many immigrants lived in overcrowded neighborhoods and apartment buildings called tenements. This Italian immigrant family (left) was photographed in their tenement building in 1910.

1800s. These immigrants came from all over Europe, including Russia, Austria, Hungary, Poland, Italy, Sweden, Norway, and Bohemia (now part of the Czech Republic). New immigrants often worked long hours at jobs that wealthier people wouldn't take. They earned low wages. A worker in a meatpacking plant might make 22 cents per hour. That would be equal to a little less than three dollars per hour today. Women and children of immigrant families worked, too. Immigrant women often found jobs as maids or nannies to the children of wealthy families. Immigrants themselves often lived in very crowded, dark, and dirty **tenement** buildings, where many families shared one building.

Immigrants mostly settled in cities, where they could find jobs in the many growing industries. City life could be hard for immigrants, but cities offered the chance to build a better life. Cities like Chicago grew rapidly. As a result, the makeup of Illinois's population changed. In 1890, most Illinoisans still lived in farming areas and small towns. By the beginning of the 1900s, more Illinoisans lived in cities.

CONFLICT

In 1910, there were 1,205,314 foreign-born **immigrants** living in Illinois. Some Illinoisans who had moved to the state earlier feared that too many immigrants were moving in. They blamed the newcomers for crime and overcrowding in big cities, as well as other problems. Some companies began requiring immigrant workers to take difficult English-language tests. They hoped the tests would drive foreign-born workers away. In 1921, new immigration laws decreased the number of people from other countries allowed into the United States.

The coming of World War II (1939–1945) caused another wave of immigrants to come to the United States from Europe. Many of these immigrants were escaping the governments of German leader Adolph Hitler and his **allies.**

The Federal Center in downtown Chicago (right) was designed by Mies van der Rohe (below). Mies moved from Germany to Chicago in 1937.

Casimir Pulaski

Illinois has one of the largest populations of Polish Americans of any state. Almost one in ten Polish Americans live in Illinois. Casimir Pulaski Day in Illinois honors a native of Poland who became a war hero in the United States. Pulaski (1748–1779) was a general who defended Poland against invading Russian forces in the 1760s and 1770s. Later, Benjamin Franklin asked Pulaski to help the United States win its independence from Great Britain. Pulaski died of a wound he received while trying to retake Savannah, Georgia, from the British. Pulaski helped train the first American **cavalry** units and became known as the "Father of the American Cavalry."

A German **architect** named Ludwig Mies van der Rohe moved to Chicago just before the war. He went on to design some of Chicago's most famous buildings, including the Federal Center downtown. An Italian scientist named Enrico Fermi moved to Chicago during the war. He performed experiments at the University of Chicago that led to the development of the atomic bomb. His experiments possibly helped the United States and its allies win the war.

Descendants of European immigrants remain an important part of Illinois's population. In 1990, more than 3 million German Americans lived in Illinois. There were also nearly 2 million Irish Americans, about 962,000 Polish Americans, and 731,000 Italian Americans, among many other groups.

The research of Italian-American Enrico Fermi (below) at the University of Chicago helped make the atomic bomb possible. The element fermium was later named in his honor.

Twentieth–Century Growth

In the 1900s, large numbers of African Americans, Asian Americans, and Latinos began moving to Illinois. Like the **immigrants** from Europe, they also helped shape Illinois.

THE GREAT MIGRATION

Beginning around 1900, African Americans from southern states like Mississippi and Alabama began moving to Illinois. This movement is sometimes called the Great Migration. African Americans came to Illinois to find work. They filled jobs in factories and mills in Chicago, Decatur, Springfield, East St. Louis, and other cities. They worked for low wages and lived in crowded

African Americans came to Illinois in the early 1900s to find work. Many helped build the towering skyscrapers of Chicago, such as the Old Tribune Building (below).

The Chicago *Defender*

The Chicago *Defender* was the most widely read newspaper for African Americans in the United States. It was founded by Robert Sengstacke Abbott (left), the son of former slaves. He graduated from Chicago's Kent College of Law in 1898, and planned to become a lawyer. However, because of racial **prejudice,** he was unable to work as a lawyer. He founded the *Defender* in 1905, and became one of the country's first African-American millionaires. The *Defender* helped thousands of African Americans make the move to Illinois. The paper often listed churches and other organizations that would help African Americans find housing and jobs in their new home. The *Defender* was later published by John Henry Sengstacke, Abbott's nephew.

African-American neighborhoods in those cities. By 1920, nearly all of the 100,000 African Americans in Chicago lived in one neighborhood called Bronzeville. Like foreign-born immigrants, the African Americans were often made to feel unwelcome in their new home. Some of the other Illinoisans complained that African Americans were taking jobs away from white workers. Conflicts between the white population and African Americans built up until violence erupted. In 1917, at least 48 people died in **riots** in East St. Louis. In 1919, almost 40 people died in a riot in Chicago.

In 2000, Chicago had the second-largest African-American population of any city in the United States. More than one million African Americans were living there. They had become a powerful political force. In 1983, they helped elect Harold Washington as Chicago's first African-American mayor. In 1992,

Harold Washington (below) was Chicago's first African-American mayor and was very popular.

Carol Moseley-Braun (above) was the first African-American woman to serve in the United States Senate.

Illinois voters made Carol Moseley-Braun the first African-American woman to serve in the United States Senate.

LATINOS IN ILLINOIS

In the second half of the 1900s, **Latinos** were one of the main **immigrant** groups moving into Illinois. Latinos are people from the Spanish-speaking countries of Mexico, Puerto Rico, Cuba, The Dominican Republic, and Guatemala. Some of these immigrants came to Illinois because jobs were hard to find in their native countries. Others were fleeing wars in **Latin America.**

Mexican Americans make up the largest group of Latinos in Illinois. Many Latinos settled in Illinois's cities, where they formed thriving neighborhoods. One of Chicago's largest Mexican-American neighborhoods is Pilsen. In fact, Pilsen is the largest Mexican-American community in the entire Midwest. It is also the home

The Mexican Fine Arts Center Museum (right) is a cultural community center in the Chicago neighborhood of Pilsen. It is also the largest Latino arts center in the United States.

Carlos Tortolero

Carlos Tortolero is the founder and executive director of the Mexican Fine Arts Center Museum in Chicago. The museum was founded in 1982, and is the largest Latino arts institution in the nation. In 2001, over 125,000 people visited the museum. This includes over 1,150 school groups from all around the Midwest.

Tortolero is originally from Nuevo Laredo, Mexico. He immigrated to Chicago at age three. From 1975 to 1987, Tortolero worked as a teacher and in other positions in the Chicago Public School system. He is currently involved in many other organizations, including the Smithsonian Institute's Center for Latino Studies and the Illinois Arts Alliance. He has also been involved in the National Association of Latino Arts and Culture and the Illinois **Humanities** Council.

Tortolero still teaches at the School of the Art Institute, Northwestern University, and in the Smithsonian Institute's Museum Awards Leadership Program. He has received numerous awards for his many efforts and accomplishments, and continues to be an inspiration to the Chicago community.

of the Mexican Fine Arts Center Museum, which is the largest Latino arts institution in the United States. The Mexican Fine Arts Center Museum displays works by Mexican-American artists and serves as a cultural

Nuevo Leon restaurant (left) serves true Mexican food. It is located in the heart of the Mexican-American community of Pilsen, in Chicago. There are many Latino-owned businesses all over the city of Chicago.

Robert Chen

Robert Chen was born in Taiwan in 1969. When he was ten years old he came to the United States with his family. When he was a boy, one of his teachers told him he should give up playing the violin. He did not give up and continued playing his whole life. In 1999, he was chosen as the concertmaster (the leader of the first violins and assistant to the conductor) of the Chicago Symphony Orchestra.

community center. Chicago is also home to groups of Puerto Rican Americans, Cuban Americans, and Guatemalan Americans. As Illinois's **Latino** population grows, so does Latino political power. In 1992, Latinos helped elect Luis Gutierrez to the U.S. House of Representatives. He was the first Latino elected to Congress from a Midwestern state.

ASIAN AMERICANS IN ILLINOIS

Large numbers of Asian Americans moved to Illinois in the second half of the 1900s. Asian Americans include people of Chinese, Filipino, Japanese, Korean, Vietnamese, and Indian origin. **Immigrants** from Cambodia, Laos, and Vietnam came to the United States to escape

Chicago's Chinatown is a busy neighborhood of restaurants, shops, and homes. By 1970, Chicago had the fourth-largest Chinese population in America.

Fazlur Khan

Fazlur Khan (1929–1982) designed some of the world's tallest buildings. He was born in what is now Bangladesh, in southern Asia, and moved to Illinois in 1952. He studied at the University of Illinois, and later taught at the Illinois Institute of Technology. He invented ways to build tall buildings without using support systems that usually took up valuable space inside the buildings. He designed Chicago's Sears Tower and John Hancock Center, two of the tallest buildings in the world.

wars in their home countries in the 1970s. Other Asians came to Illinois to attend universities. University towns like Champaign and Normal are home to large Asian-American populations. Many Asians also settled in Chicago and its **suburbs.** Chicago actually has a thriving Chinatown and other neighborhoods of Chinese Americans, Korean Americans, and Vietnamese Americans.

FROM FARM TO CITY

Some of the largest population shifts in Illinois history were the result of people moving from one place to another within the state. This is known as internal

The Sears Tower (right) was designed by Fazlur Khan and was completed in 1974. It is the largest private office building in the world.

migration. For example, there has been a steady shift in population from **rural** areas of Illinois to cities. In the 1800s, Illinois was mainly a rural state. Most of its population lived in small towns and on farms. But for over one hundred years, more and more Illinoisans have lived in cities. There are many reasons why city populations have increased. Inventors produced farm equipment that could do much of the work on farms. As a result, farms required fewer workers. More people began moving to cities in search of jobs and education. Farm counties lost population, even as the state's total population increased. In 1990, only two of every ten Illinoisans lived in a farming area.

Over the last 100 years, many Illinoisans have left rural towns for big cities and suburbs. They often move in order to find jobs. As this happens, some rural towns are almost totally abandoned (below).

GROWTH OF THE SUBURBS

By the start of the twenty-first century, Illinois's population had shifted to the **suburbs.**

Naperville's Riverwalk along the DuPage River (left) is one of its many attractions that brings people there to live. There is more space for each person to enjoy in many suburbs. There are also still some areas of nature. These are some of the reasons why Chicago's suburbs grew so much between 1990 and 2000.

The first suburbs began appearing in the 1800s. They were located along railroads outside cities like Chicago. Suburbs became more popular in the second half of the 1900s. In the 1940s and 1950s, automobiles became more affordable and more common. At the same time, new highways and roads made travel easier and quicker. As a result, people no longer had to live near railroad lines or in big cities. Instead, they could drive to work in the city from their homes in the suburbs. The suburbs also offered large new schools and open space for raising families. Suburban populations grew quickly. By 2000, many Illinois suburbs had grown as large as medium-sized cities. Chicago suburbs like Aurora and Naperville were among the fastest-growing places in Illinois.

The Twenty-First Century

Of the fifty United States, Illinois ranks 24th in land area. However, Illinois is the fifth largest state in population. At the start of the twenty-first century, 12,419,293 people lived in Illinois. That is an increase over the number of people in Illinois just ten years earlier. Between 1990 and 2000, Illinois's population increased by nearly one million people.

A History of Growth

Since Illinois became a state in 1818, its population has been growing almost constantly. In the state's early years, it was one of the fastest growing places in the world. Between 1820 and 1830, the state's population boomed from 55,162 to 157,445. Many

Of Illinois's top ten most populated cities, all but Peoria saw an increase in population between 1990 and 2000.

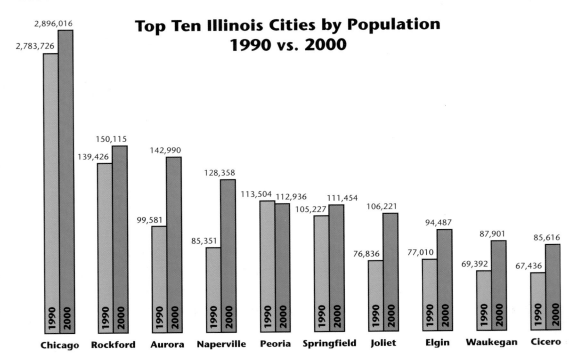

**Top Ten Illinois Cities by Population
1990 vs. 2000**

City	1990	2000
Chicago	2,783,726	2,896,016
Rockford	139,426	150,115
Aurora	99,581	142,990
Naperville	85,351	128,358
Peoria	113,504	112,936
Springfield	105,227	111,454
Joliet	76,836	106,221
Elgin	77,010	94,487
Waukegan	69,392	87,901
Cicero	67,436	85,616

Illinois Population by County

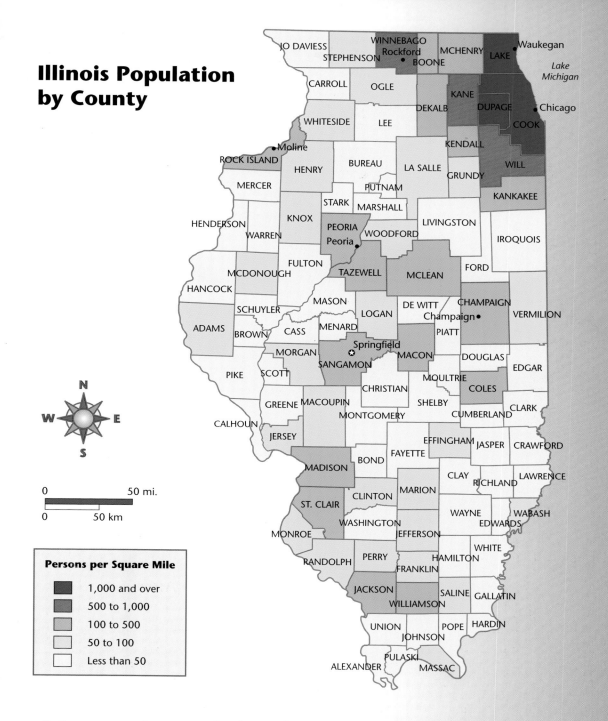

Persons per Square Mile

- 1,000 and over
- 500 to 1,000
- 100 to 500
- 50 to 100
- Less than 50

of those people came looking for good farmland, like Abraham Lincoln's family.

Illinois continued to grow steadily. In the first few decades of the 1900s, Illinois grew by nearly one million people every ten years. Many of those people came from Europe or the American South looking for jobs in the factories that were appearing all over Illinois.

The U.S. Census

The best source for information about the population of Illinois is the census taken by the United States government. A census is a counting of the people who live in a certain place. The United States government conducts a census every ten years. The first was in 1790. Besides counting the people living in the United States, the census provides information about those people. People fill out census forms that ask for information about their age, their race, what languages they speak, and how much money they make, to name just a few examples. By comparing the result of one census with the results of an earlier census, we can gain an understanding of how the population of a place such as Illinois has changed over the years.

Only in the 1980s did Illinois fail to have an increase in population. During those years, the flow of new residents into the state slowed. The prices for crops grown in Illinois dropped, so farmers suffered. Many Illinois factories closed in the 1970s and 1980s, costing people their jobs. Between 1973 and 1993, the number of manufacturing plants in Chicago alone dropped from 7,330 to 4,720. With fewer jobs available in factories and hard times on farms, people were not as anxious to move to Illinois.

Chicago (right) gained in population between 1990 and 2000. This was the first time it gained population in about 50 years. According to the 2000 U.S. census, 2,896,016 people live in Chicago. That's an increase of 112,290 people from 1990.

GROWING CITIES

At the start of the twenty-first century, Illinois was steadily growing again. **Immigrants** continued to move to Illinois from **Latin America,** Asia, and other parts of the world. People in other areas of the United States moved to Illinois, as well. Like people throughout Illinois's history, they came to find work and a better life.

Not only did the state's population increase, but its largest city grew, as well. Like many big cities, Chicago had been slowly losing population since 1950. However, the 2000 census showed an increase in population in Chicago for the first time in 50 years.

Chicago's **suburbs** also grew, according to the 2000 census. In fact, the ten fastest growing cities or villages in Illinois are all in the Chicago area. Suburbs like Aurora and Naperville grew so quickly that they now rank among the largest cities in Illinois. Only a few cities outside the Chicago area experienced similar growth. Bloomington, in central Illinois, grew to a population of 64,808. This is an increase of over 12,000 from 1990. That made it the

The central Illinois city of Bloomington (left) continues to grow. It gained over 12,000 people between 1990 and 2000. A portion of Bloomington's population attends Illinois State University and Illinois Wesleyan University there.

31

Growing Populations

A growing population is considered a sign of a nice place to live. It means the economy there is healthy. It also usually means the area's schools, parks, and other public places make it a nice place for families to live. However, population growth also brings problems. When too many people want to move to a city or town, the natural surroundings can suffer. New homes and businesses take up land that is home to plants and animals. As a result, plants and animals are often pushed out of the area or destroyed. A city's rapid growth can also bring problems for the people who live and work there. Area roads can become so clogged with cars that people spend hours just traveling to and from work.

seventeenth largest city in Illinois. Normal grew to a population of 45,388, which is an increase of over 5,000. The Southern Illinois towns of Godfrey and Edwardsville also grew. Godfrey's population increased from 5,436 to 18,288. Edwardsville's increased from 14,579 to 21,491.

Illinois is likely to keep growing, too. The U.S. Census Bureau estimates that by 2015, nearly 13 million people will live in Illinois. It also says that by 2025, the state will have grown by about another 400,000 people.

ILLINOIS: A PORTRAIT

The 2000 census showed a picture of the people living in Illinois at the start of the new century. They belonged to a wide range of **ethnic** groups. The more than 9 million **Caucasian** people made up the largest group. African Americans made up the next largest group, with 1,876,875 people. Close behind were **Latinos,** with 1,530,262 people. The largest group of Latinos in Illinois are Mexican Americans. In 2000, the Mexican-American population of

Illinois Population by Race: 1990 vs. 2000

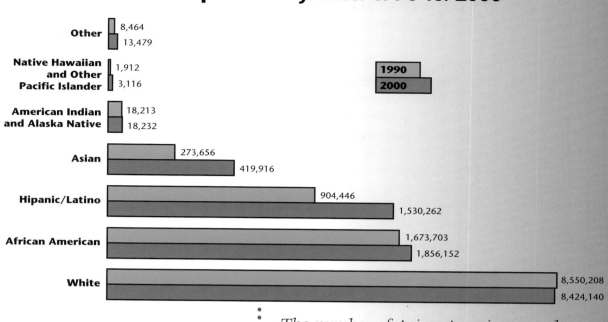

Race	1990	2000
Other	8,464	13,479
Native Hawaiian and Other Pacific Islander	1,912	3,116
American Indian and Alaska Native	18,213	18,232
Asian	273,656	419,916
Hipanic/Latino	904,446	1,530,262
African American	1,673,703	1,856,152
White	8,550,208	8,424,140

Illinois was 1,144,390. Illinois was also home to 423,603 Asian Americans in 2000, including 124,723 people of Indian **descent,** 86,298 people of Filipino descent, and 76,725 people of Chinese descent.

The number of Asian Americans and Latinos living in Illinois increased greatly between 1990 and 2000.

When filling out the 2000 census form, many people wrote that they considered themselves part of many ethnic groups. This shows that people are welcoming the different ethnic groups of Illinois into their lives and families. People are learning to embrace cultural **diversity** and place less importance on ethnic differences.

People still come to Illinois from all over the world. Today, nearly one of every five residents speaks a language other than English in the home. No matter what language they speak, these people all help shape Illinois. Their languages, beliefs, and **customs** are a welcome part of the Illinois way of life.

Illinois's growing population is a sign that it is a good place to live and raise families. And, Illinois families are increasingly diverse in their makeup.

Illinois Achievers

Addams, Jane (1860–1935), reformer. Addams worked to improve the lives of poor people in Chicago and the rest of the world. Born in Cedarville, Illinois, she graduated from Rockford College in 1881. She was part of the first generation of American women to attend college. In 1889, she moved into a home in the **slums** of Chicago and turned it into a community center for poor people. She named the home Hull House. At Hull House, Addams provided services and support for the poor people that the rest of society often ignored. At Hull House, poor Chicagoans could attend classes, exercise in the gymnasium, and read books in the library. Addams spoke out against child labor, overcrowding in cities, and unclean conditions. In 1931, she received the **Nobel** Peace **Prize** for her work.

Jane Addams at Hull House

Armstrong, Louis (1900–1971), musician. Armstrong helped shape jazz music in its early years. His original style of trumpet playing has inspired generations of musicians. Born in New Orleans, Louisiana, he began playing in bands on riverboats along the Mississippi River. In 1922, he moved to Chicago, where he became a featured performer in the most popular bands of the time.

Benny, Jack (1894–1974), comedian. Benny was a star of radio and television comedy shows for more than 30 years. Raised in Waukegan, Illinois, he was first heard on the radio in 1932.

Louis Armstrong

Berwanger, Jay (1914–), athlete. In 1935, Berwanger won the first Heisman Trophy, which is the award given to college football's most outstanding player of the year. He played football at the University of Chicago.

Black Hawk (1767–1838), Native American leader. Black Hawk led a group of Sauk and Fox in the last effort to regain their village sites from white settlers in Illinois. In 1832, he and his supporters fought a desperate war, now known as the Black Hawk War, against the U.S. Army and Illinois militia. The Native Americans were defeated and driven from Illinois for the last time.

Gwendolyn Brooks

Brooks, Gwendolyn (1917–2000), poet. Brooks wrote poems about the everyday lives of African Americans in cities like Chicago. She was the first African-American poet to win the **Pulitzer Prize.** In 1968, she was named **poet laureate** of Illinois.

Burnham, Daniel (1846–1912), **architect.** Burnham was chief architect for the 1893 World's Columbian Exposition in Chicago. He designed several famous buildings in Chicago in the late 1800s. His 1907 Plan for Chicago called for many open, natural spaces in the city, especially along the lakefront.

Byrne, Jane (1934–), politician. Byrne was elected as Chicago's first female mayor in 1979. She served one term.

Cabrini, St. Frances Xavier (1850–1917), **missionary.** Cabrini established hospitals, orphanages, and schools for poor Italian **immigrants** in New York City and Chicago. She also founded the Missionary Sisters of the Sacred Heart in the United States. She was the first U.S. citizen to be named a **saint.**

Hillary Rodham Clinton

Clinton, Hillary Rodham (1947–), politician. Clinton won election to the United States Senate while her husband, Bill Clinton, was serving as president of the United States. Raised in Park Ridge, Illinois, she is the only first lady to have been elected to a political office. As first lady, she spoke out for the protection of the rights of children around the world. In 2001, she took office as a U.S. senator for New York.

Daley, Richard J. (1902–1976), politician. Daley was mayor of Chicago for 21 years, from 1955 until his death. He encouraged the building of downtown skyscrapers, highways, housing projects for the poor, and college **campuses.**

Daley, Richard M. (1942–), politician. Daley followed in his father's footsteps as mayor of Chicago. Elected three times beginning in 1991, he was Chicago's mayor at the turn of the twenty-first century.

Davis, Miles (1926–1991), musician. Davis mixed jazz and rock music to create new styles of music. Born in Alton, Illinois, he became an accomplished jazz trumpet player. He was a pioneer in the style of jazz called "cool jazz."

Deere, John (1804–1886), inventor. Deere invented a steel plow in 1837 that made it easier for farmers to work the prairies of Illinois. His plows cut through the tough roots of prairie grasses, making the soil ready for corn and other crops. In 1847, he established a factory in Moline, Illinois, to manufacture the plows. Deere's steel plow allowed settlers to come to Illinois and successfully farm the prairie land.

John Deere

Du Sable, Jean Baptiste Point (1745?–1818), pioneer. Du Sable pioneered the settlement that eventually became Chicago. A Haitian trader, he built a trading post that became the center of the first permanent settlement on the banks of the Chicago River, near Lake Michigan.

Jean Baptiste Point Du Sable

Fermi, Enrico (1901–1954), scientist. Fermi performed experiments at the University of Chicago that led to the development of the atomic bomb. He left Italy to help the United States during World War II (1939–1945). He later became a U.S. citizen and a professor at the University of Chicago.

Friedan, Betty (1921–), writer. Friedan helped found the National Organization for Women in 1966. The group worked to secure equal rights for women. A native of Peoria, Illinois, Friedan has written books and articles about modern women's problems.

Goodman, Benny (1909–1986), musician. Goodman became known as the "King of Swing" because his clarinet playing made the style of jazz called "swing music" popular. As a boy, he studied clarinet at Jane Addams's Hull House in Chicago.

Grange, Harold "Red" (1903–1991), athlete. Grange was professional football's first star. Raised in Wheaton, Illinois, his talent as a running back at the University of Illinois made him nationally known. He joined the Chicago Bears in 1925, bringing in record crowds wherever he played.

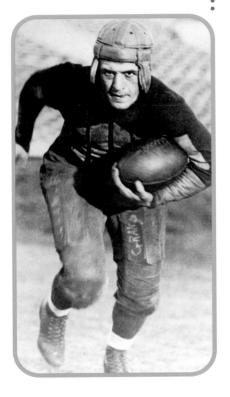

Harold "Red" Grange

Grant, Ulysses Simpson (1822–1885), politician and soldier. Grant commanded Union troops in the Civil War (1861–1865) and was later elected president of the United States. He was a graduate of the United States Military Academy at West Point, New York. Grant served in the Mexican War (1846–1848). He was a store clerk in Galena, Illinois, when the Civil War started. He was made a general in 1861 and given command of all Union troops in 1864. His military leadership led to a Union victory after four long years of war. He accepted the surrender of Confederate General

Robert E. Lee in 1865. Grant ran for the presidency and was elected in 1868. He served two terms as president.

Halas, George (1895–1983), athlete. Halas helped start the National Football League (NFL) in 1920. He played for, coached, and owned the Chicago Bears. The team's fans knew him as "Papa Bear."

Hemingway, Ernest (1899–1961), writer. Hemingway won the **Nobel Prize** for Literature in 1954. Born in Oak Park, Illinois, he became one of the most respected novelists and short-story writers of his time.

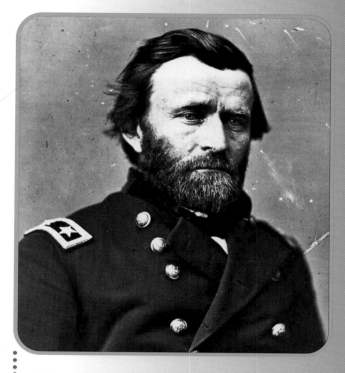

Ulysses Simpson Grant

Jemison, Mae (1956–), astronaut. Jemison became the first female African-American astronaut in 1988. Raised in Chicago, she studied medicine and practiced medicine with the Peace Corps in West Africa. In 1992, she spent a week in space aboard the space shuttle *Endeavour.*

Mae Jemison

Johnson, John H. (1918–), publisher. Johnson publishes books and magazines, such as *Ebony*, especially for an African-American audience. His Johnson Publishing Co., based in Chicago, is the world's largest African-American-owned publishing company.

Jolliet, Louis (1645–1700), explorer. Jolliet was one of the first white men to visit Illinois. In 1673, with Jacques Marquette, he led a voyage down the Mississippi River. This voyage took them from present-day Wisconsin to present-day Arkansas. On their return trip, Jolliet and Marquette traveled up the Illinois River and passed the future site of Chicago.

Jordan, Michael (1963–), athlete. Jordan led the Chicago Bulls to six National Basketball Association (NBA) championships. His skills and accomplishments made him one of the world's best-known and most-admired athletes. In 2000, he became partial owner of the Washington Wizards of the NBA. In 2001, he gave up that ownership and decided to return to basketball as an NBA player for the Wizards.

Joyner-Kersee, Jackie (1962–), athlete. Joyner-Kersee won three gold medals in track events at the 1984 and 1988 Olympics. She was born in East St. Louis, Illinois.

La Salle, René-Robert Cavalier, Sieur de (1643–1687), explorer. La Salle led an **expedition** down the Illinois and Mississippi Rivers in 1682. He claimed all the land drained by the rivers for his native France. He built several **forts** on the Illinois River—one near present-day Peoria, Illinois, and another near Starved Rock.

Lincoln, Abraham (1809–1865), politician. Lincoln was the first Illinoisan elected president of the

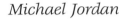

Michael Jordan

United States. His leadership during the Civil War (1861–1865) carried the country through one of its most troubled times. Lincoln was born in Kentucky but moved to Illinois with his family when he was 21. He lived first in New Salem, Illinois, and then in Springfield. As a young man, he worked as a **surveyor,** store clerk, boatman, farmhand, and even served as postmaster of New Salem. All the while, he continued to teach himself **grammar** and the law. He became an **attorney** and was

Abraham Lincoln

elected to the Illinois state legislature in 1834. He served four terms there and one term in the U.S. Congress (1847–1849). In the 1850s, he twice ran unsuccessfully for the U.S. Senate. In 1858, he and opponent Stephen A. Douglas debated seven times in towns all over the state of Illinois. Lincoln's arguments against the spread of slavery earned him respect and fame, even though he lost that election. In 1860, he ran for the presidency and won. By that time, the nation was bitterly divided over the issue of slavery. Seven Southern states left the Union by the time Lincoln was **inaugurated.** As president, Lincoln signed the Emancipation Proclamation in 1863, which ended slavery in the **Confederate** states. He led the nation through the Civil War, but did not live to see the Southern and Northern states reunited. He was shot by John Wilkes Booth on April 14, 1865, and died April 15. His body was carried by train to Springfield, Illinois, where he was buried. Only months after his death, the Thirteenth Amendment to the Constitution abolished slavery everywhere in the United States.

Elijah Lovejoy

Lovejoy, Elijah Parish (1802–1837), publisher and **abolitionist.** Lovejoy published a newspaper in Alton, Illinois, and campaigned against slavery. For more information on Lovejoy, turn to page 13.

Marquette, Jacques (1637–1675), explorer and **missionary.** Marquette visited Illinois with Louis Jolliet on their historic trip down the Mississippi River in 1673. For more information on Marquette, turn to page 7.

Explorer Jacques Marquette

McCormick, Cyrus (1809–1884), inventor. McCormick built the first successful reaper, a machine for cutting grain. In 1847, he opened a factory in Chicago to manufacture reapers. These reapers made it possible for Illinois farmers to work more efficiently and quickly than ever before.

Cyrus McCormick

Mies van der Rohe, Ludwig (1886–1969), **architect.** Mies designed many of the buildings on the Illinois Institute of Technology **campus.** His designs for buildings in Chicago set the style for many of the glass and steel skyscrapers built around the world in the 1960s and 1970s. You can look at one of his buildings on page 18.

Reagan, Ronald (1911–), politician. Reagan was elected 40th president of the United States in 1980. He was born in Tampico, Illinois, and grew up in Dixon. He attended Eureka College in Eureka, Illinois, where he played football and was active in theater. He was class president in his last year of college. He worked as a sportscaster in Iowa, then began a career as a movie actor in Hollywood, California. He made more than 50 films. In 1966, he was elected governor of California. In 1980, he became the first movie actor to be elected president of the United States. He served two terms and remained popular for most of his

Ronald Reagan, the 40th president of the United States

time in office. After he retired, he announced that he suffered from Alzheimer's disease. Alzheimer's affects a person's mind and causes a loss of memory.

Sandburg, Carl (1878–1967), writer. Sandburg wrote poems about the accomplishments of ordinary Americans. He was born in Galesburg, Illinois. His **biography** of Abraham Lincoln won the **Pulitzer Prize** for history in 1940.

Joseph Smith

Smith, Joseph (1805–1844), church leader. Smith founded the **Mormon** religion and led his followers to Illinois in 1839. They settled in Nauvoo, Illinois, before moving west to Utah. To learn more about Joseph Smith and the Mormons, see pages 13–14.

Spalding, Albert G. (1850–1915), athlete. Spalding was an early baseball star who helped make the game popular around the world. He was born in Byron, Illinois, and played for and managed Chicago's National League team—the Chicago White Stockings—in 1876, when they won the championship. Later that year, he opened a sporting goods store with his brother J. Walter Spalding. This eventually grew into the famous Spalding sporting goods company.

Stevenson, Adlai E. (1900–1965), politician. Stevenson was elected governor of Illinois in 1948 by a record number of votes. He twice ran unsuccessfully for president of the United States (1952 and 1956). He was also United States ambassador to the United Nations from 1961 until his death.

Sullivan, Louis (1856–1924), **architect.** Sullivan was the architect for several famous buildings in Chicago. He was one of the architects who helped rebuild Chicago in the years after the Great Chicago Fire (1871). His ideas helped shape modern architecture.

Thompson, James R. (1936–), politician. Thompson was the first governor of Illinois to win election to four consecutive (one right after the other) terms in office. He worked to improve the state's highways and increase funding for healthcare facilities.

Washington, Harold (1922–1987), politician. Washington was elected the first African-American mayor of Chicago in 1983. He also served two terms in the U.S. House of Representatives (1980–1983). As mayor of Chicago, he worked to improve city government and create greater opportunities for the poor.

Harold Washington

Willard, Frances (1839–1898), reformer. Willard worked in the late 1800s to give women the right to vote. She graduated from Northwestern Female College in Evanston, Illinois. In 1879, she became president of the Women's **Christian** Temperance Union, a national women's group that spoke out against alcohol.

Winfrey, Oprah (1954–), television host, actor, media executive. Winfrey runs a Chicago-based television production company called Harpo Productions. Since 1985, she has hosted one of television's most popular daily talk shows. She also acts in movies and publishes a magazine called *O*.

Oprah Winfrey

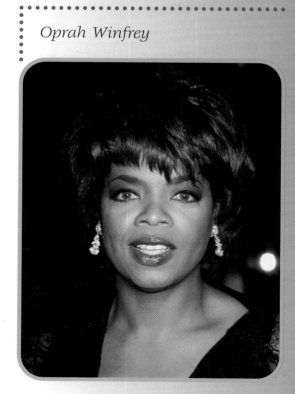

Wright, Frank Lloyd (1867–1959), architect. Wright invented the "Prairie style" of architecture. He drew inspiration for his buildings from the flat prairie landscapes of Illinois and the Midwest. He designed many homes and public buildings in Chicago and Oak Park, Illinois.

Glossary

abolition outlawing of slavery. An abolitionist is a person who worked to outlaw slavery.

ally person or group of people who promise to help someone else

architect person who designs buildings and gives advice on their construction

attorney person who gives others advice on law or represents them in a law court

biography book that tells the life story of a person

bison also sometimes called a buffalo; large, shaggy-maned mammal with short horns and a hump

campus land around a college

Catholic of the Roman Catholic faith, which is the Christian church governed by the pope in Rome

Caucasian member of the Caucasoid race; people with white skin are often also called Caucasian, especially in the U.S. Census

cavalry part of a military force that operates on horseback

Christian of a religion that came from Jesus Christ and is based on the Bible; Eastern, Roman Catholic, and Protestant churches are Christian

Confederate belonging to the Confederate States of America, which were the southern states in rebellion during the Civil War (1861–1865)

custom something that a person or group of people usually does; something that has been done for a long time and has become a normal habit

descendant person who has come from an older relative, or ancestor

descent description of the relatives that a person has come from; for instance, a person could be of Irish descent, meaning his or her older relatives were originally from Ireland

discriminate treat someone differently because of a person's race, religion, or other characteristic

diversity variety

ethnic belonging to a certain group of people who speak the same language and have the same customs

expedition organized journey of a group of people

famine period during which food is scarce in a certain place

fort strong building used for defense against enemy attack

French and Indian War war that took place in America from 1754 to 1763, between the French and their Native American friends on one side, and the British and their Native American friends on the other

grammar system of rules for speaking and writing a language

humanities studies that deal with human relations and thought, such as literature, philosophy, music, and art

immigrant person who comes into a foreign country to make a new home

inaugurated publicly and formally placed in office through a ceremony

Latin America parts of North, South, and Central America where Spanish and related languages are spoken

Latino a person from a Latin American country or who speaks Spanish; the term Hispanic is also sometimes used to describe such a person

Lutheran Church Christian church founded by Martin Luther in the 1500s

missionary person who travels to spread his or her religious faith. A mission is a place where missionaries live and work.

Mississippian Culture civilization that thrived along the Mississippi River around C.E. 1000

Mormon member of the Church of Jesus Christ of Latter-day Saints, which is the church founded by Joseph Smith

Nobel Prize one of a group of prizes, including the Nobel Peace Prize, awarded each year for achievements in different fields

poet laureate poet honored for excellence by a state or nation

prejudice unfavorable opinion formed without good reason

Presbyterian Church Protestant Christian church governed by presbyters, or elders of equal rank

Pulitzer Prize one of a group of prizes awarded each year for works of journalism, history, and biography

riot great disorder, confusion, or violence by a crowd of people; to take part in a riot

rural having to do with the country or farmland

saint very holy person honored by a church after his or her death

slum crowded and poor section of a city

starvation process of dying of hunger

suburb city or town just outside a larger city

surveyor person who measures and inspects a piece of land

tenement old, crowded apartment in the poor part of a city

territory area of land in the United States that is not organized as a state, but has its own local government

Woodland Culture civilization that thrived in North America around 1000 B.C.E.

More Books to Read

Bial, Raymond. *Where Lincoln Walked.* New York: Walker and Company, 1998.

Boekhoff, P. M. and Stuart A. Kallen. *Illinois.* Farmington Hills, Mich.: Gale Group, 2001.

Harmon, Daniel E. *Jolliet and Marquette: Explorers of the Mississippi River.* Broomall, Pa.: Chelsea House, 2001.

Marsh, Carole. *Illinois History! Surprising Secrets about Our State's Founding Mothers, Fathers and Kids!* Peachtree City, Ga.: Gallopade International, 1996.

Simon, Charnan. *Jane Addams: Pioneer Social Worker.* Danbury, Conn.: Children's Press, 1998.

Fiction:

Edge, Laura B. *A Personal Tour of Hull House.* Minneapolis, Minn.: Lerner Publishing, 2001.

Hoobler, Dorothy and Thomas Hoobler. *Florence Robinson: The Story of a World War I Girl.* Parsippany, N.J.: Silver Burdett, 1997.

Index

About the Author

Andrew Santella lives in Trout Valley, Illinois, and is a lifelong resident of the state of Illinois. He is the author of 25 nonfiction books for children. He also writes for publications such as *GQ* and the *New York Times Book Review.*